Macroeconomics Made Easy For Beginners

Roggie Clark

Avoid Credit Card Debt With This Book

Are you tired of living paycheck to paycheck? Drowning in interest rates and minimum payments that never seem to shrink your balance? *Understanding & Overcoming Credit Card Debt* is your roadmap to financial freedom.

https://www.amazon.com/dp/B0F3WCVWG8

Avoid Wasting Money On Crypto With This Book

Whether you're curious, cautious, or ready to invest, this book breaks down complex topics into plain language and cuts through the noise, buzzwords, and get-rich-quick schemes.

https://www.amazon.com/Think-Before-You-Crypto-Understanding-ebook/dp/B0F3YQ1L2Q

Learn How To Invest in Gold Bars With This Book

Whether you're new to investing or seeking to diversify your portfolio, this beginner-friendly guide will give you the knowledge and confidence to invest in gold, and other precious metals.

https://www.amazon.com/Ultimate-Investing-Buying-Guide-Beginners-ebook/dp/B0F1KWWDXG

Learn How To Invest in Silver With This Book

Whether you're approaching retirement or already enjoying it, protecting and growing your wealth is critical. The Ultimate Silver Investing & Buying Guide For Beginners is your clear, no-nonsense guide to incorporating silver into your wealth-building strategy.

https://www.amazon.com/Ultimate-Silver-Investing-Buying-Beginners-ebook

Copyright

Title: Macroeconomics Made Easy For Beginners
Author: Roggie Clark

Disclaimer

The views and opinions expressed in this book are those of the author and do not necessarily reflect the official policy or position of any individual, company, or organization cited or referenced in the text. The author is not affiliated with any of the individuals, companies, or organizations mentioned in the text, nor does the author receive any form of compensation for citing or referencing them.

The professional information in this text is distributed on an "as is" basis, without warranty. While every precaution has been taken in the preparation of the text, neither the author nor the publisher shall have any liability to any person or entity with respect to any loss or damage caused or alleged to be caused directly or indirectly by the instructions contained in this text or by the computer software and hardware products described in it.

The author nor the publisher does not guarantee any specific results or outcomes, and the information provided in this text should not be construed as professional advice. Readers should always consult with a qualified professional before making any significant changes to their website or business.

By reading this text, you agree that the author nor the publisher is responsible for any direct, indirect, incidental, or consequential damages that may arise from the use of the information provided. You assume full responsibility for any actions taken based on the information presented in this text.

College Or University Usage

I recommend that college deans and professors consider this book for their curriculum; as well as a resource for your students to use for their own research. If you are interested in using the book for your course or having your bookstore source it for students to purchase, you can reach out to me directly.

Please email me at **bounceranksseo@gmail.com**. In your email, please include the following information:

- Your name
- The school you represent
- The class size you are teaching
- The length of your course (e.g. 6-week course, 12-week course, etc.)
- Any other important information I should know

My administrative assistant will email you back within 24 - 48 hours with rates, and an information sheet to use for your class.

Table of Contents

Introduction

Macroeconomics often feels confusing, abstract, or disconnected from real life. Headlines talk about inflation, recessions, interest rates, trade wars, and job numbers, yet many people are left wondering what any of it actually means for their lives, their businesses, or their future.

This book was written to change that.

Macroeconomics is not just about charts, formulas, or government reports. It is about **patterns**. It explains why prices rise, why jobs appear and disappear, why policies help in one moment and fail in another, and why economic conditions can feel strong on paper while everyday life feels more difficult.

At its core, macroeconomics studies the economy as a whole. It looks at **economic cycles**, **inflation**, **trade**, **policy decisions**, **employment**, and **productivity**, not as isolated topics, but as interconnected forces. When one shifts, the others respond. Understanding those relationships is what turns economic noise into useful insight.

This book is designed for beginners, but it does not talk down to you. You will not find heavy math, complex formulas, or academic jargon. Instead, you will find clear explanations, real world examples, and honest discussions about trade offs and limitations. Where economic debates exist, they are acknowledged. Where data can mislead, that reality is addressed directly.

You will learn why:

- Economic expansions and recessions are recurring, not random
- Inflation is driven by more than just corporate behavior or policy decisions
- Trade and globalization create both opportunity and disruption
- Economic indicators inform decisions but never tell the whole story
- No single economic school of thought explains everything
- Monetary and fiscal policy are powerful, but imperfect tools
- Job numbers alone do not define economic well being

More importantly, you will learn how to **think macroeconomically**, how to zoom out, recognize patterns, question assumptions, and connect economic events to real outcomes.

For students, this book provides a strong foundation for understanding economics beyond memorization. For business owners and marketers, it offers a framework for making better strategic decisions in uncertain environments. For everyday readers, it offers clarity in a world where economic messaging is often overwhelming or contradictory.

Macroeconomics is not about predicting the future perfectly. It is about understanding the system well enough to navigate change intelligently.

That is what this book is here to help you do.

Chapter 1: Economic Cycles

As you move through this book, you will begin to see that understanding economics is not just about saving money or memorizing definitions. It is about learning how to **anticipate economic shifts**, recognize patterns in decision making, and understand how businesses and policymakers respond to changing conditions. When you understand these patterns, you are better positioned to plan ahead and recognize opportunities that others may miss.

This chapter begins our focus on **macroeconomics**, the study of the economy as a whole. Here, we explore **economic cycles** and how they influence business activity, government policy, and consumer behavior over time.

Different Economic Cycles

Economic cycles, also known as **business cycles**, describe the recurring rise and fall of economic activity within an economy. These cycles are not random. While no two cycles look exactly the same, most economies move through four recognizable stages: **expansion**, **peak**, **contraction**, and **trough**.

Understanding where an economy sits within this cycle helps explain changes in employment, spending habits, investment decisions, and policy responses.

Why Economic Cycles Matter

Understanding **economic cycles** is important because these shifts affect far more than abstract charts or government reports. Economic cycles influence **prices**, **wages**, **job security**, and the overall availability of opportunities in the economy.

For businesses, recognizing where the economy sits in a cycle helps guide decisions about hiring, expansion, pricing, and investment. During expansions, companies are more willing to take risks and grow. During contractions, they often focus on cost control, efficiency, and survival.

For policymakers, economic cycles shape decisions around **Monetary policy** and **Fiscal policy**. Central banks may raise or lower interest rates depending on economic conditions, while governments adjust spending and taxation to stabilize growth or stimulate demand.

For consumers, cycles influence confidence and behavior. People tend to spend more freely when employment is strong and incomes are rising, while uncertainty during downturns often leads to reduced spending and increased saving.

By understanding economic cycles, individuals can better interpret economic news, anticipate changes in the business environment, and make more informed financial and career decisions over time.

Expansion Phase

During the **Expansion phase**, economic activity increases steadily. Growth is often measured by **GDP (Gross Domestic Product)**, which represents the total value of goods and services produced within a country. As GDP rises, **consumer confidence**, or how optimistic people feel about the economy, typically improves.

Higher confidence leads to increased spending and investment. Businesses respond by expanding operations, increasing production, and hiring more workers. As a result, **unemployment**, the share of people actively seeking work but unable to find it, usually remains low during this phase.

A clear historical example occurred after the **2008 financial crisis**, when many global economies entered a long period of recovery and expansion as financial systems stabilized and confidence returned.

An even more extended example is the **post–World War II economic boom**, spanning roughly from the mid 1940s through the 1960s. Returning soldiers, government investment in infrastructure, and strong consumer demand fueled one of the longest growth periods in U.S. history. Suburban development expanded rapidly, car ownership increased, and manufacturing and service industries flourished.

Similarly, during the 2010s, the U.S. experienced a record length expansion following the Great Recession. This period was marked by steady job growth, rising financial markets, and rapid expansion in technology driven sectors such as cloud computing and e commerce.

Peak Phase

The **Peak phase** represents the highest point of economic activity. At this stage, the economy is operating at or near full capacity. Growth begins to slow, and **Inflation**, the general increase in prices across the economy, often accelerates due to strong demand.

During peaks, **wages**, or earnings, tend to rise as businesses compete for workers. However, this phase can also be marked by excessive optimism, speculative behavior, and risk taking.

The **dot com bubble of the late 1990s** illustrates this stage well. Many internet based companies attracted massive investment despite weak or nonexistent business models. When it became clear these firms could not generate sustainable profits, the bubble burst in 2000, triggering sharp market declines and business failures.

Another example occurred in the **U.S. housing market during the mid 2000s**. By 2006, home prices had reached extreme levels, driven by easy credit and speculative buying. This overconfidence marked the peak just before the 2008 financial collapse.

More recently, some economists and investors have suggested that rapid investment in **artificial intelligence** may represent another potential bubble, as of 2025, reflecting familiar patterns seen near past economic peaks.

Contraction Phase

After the peak, the economy enters the **Contraction phase**, commonly referred to as a **Recession**. A recession involves a sustained decline in economic activity, typically lasting several months, and is characterized by falling GDP, reduced spending, and rising unemployment.

The **2008 financial crisis** offers a clear example. In the years leading up to the crash, banks issued high risk mortgages to borrowers with weak or nonexistent credit profiles. These loans were packaged into complex financial products such as **mortgage backed securities** and **synthetic collateralized debt obligations**, which were difficult to value and widely sold to investors.

When homeowners began defaulting on their loans, these securities rapidly lost value, triggering widespread financial instability. Credit markets froze, borrowing became difficult, businesses closed, and job losses spread globally.

In extreme cases, contractions deepen into a **Depression**, which is far more severe and long lasting. The **Great Depression of the 1930s** was driven by multiple factors, including the 1929 stock market crash, widespread bank failures, and collapsing confidence. At its worst, unemployment in the United States reached approximately 25 percent, and the global economy suffered for nearly a decade.

Another modern example occurred during the **COVID 19 pandemic in 2020**, which triggered one of the fastest and most synchronized global contractions in history. Lockdowns, travel restrictions, and supply chain disruptions caused GDP to fall sharply worldwide. In the U.S., unemployment surged to nearly 15 percent in April 2020. Although governments responded with large stimulus efforts, the episode demonstrated how quickly unexpected shocks can push economies into contraction.

Stagflation

In some situations, economies experience **Stagflation**, a rare condition where **high inflation**, **high unemployment**, and **slow or stagnant growth** occur simultaneously.

Stagflation is particularly difficult to manage because policies aimed at reducing inflation, such as raising interest rates, often increase unemployment. At the same time, efforts to reduce unemployment through government spending can worsen inflation.

A well known example occurred during the **1970s oil crisis**, when sharp increases in oil prices raised production costs, slowed economic growth, and drove inflation higher at the same time.

Another similar example of Stagflation is being observed in 2025, specifically in the United States, while the rapid expansion of artificial intelligence has been praised for it's influence in the stock market, the expansion of AI has also lead to widespread job loss.

As corporations, and even small businesses rapidly automate, this drastic increase in unemployement, along with high inflation caused by laxed tariff policies, unrestricted immigration, and record monetary stimulus from the 2020 pandemic by central banks (quantitative easing). Has lead to another instance of stagflation, and recession, and even depression like indicators flashing red.

Trough

The **Trough** represents the lowest point in the economic cycle. At this stage, economic activity has bottomed out, confidence remains weak, and unemployment is typically elevated. However, the trough also marks the turning point toward recovery.

As conditions stabilize, businesses and consumers slowly regain confidence, laying the foundation for renewed growth and the next expansion phase.

One example is **1938 in the United States**, which marked the trough of the Great Depression. Policies introduced under Franklin D. Roosevelt's New Deal in 1933, combined with gradual improvements in consumer confidence, helped the economy begin a slow recovery, but it wasn't officially until the United States entered World War II that the Great Depression had ended. Massive government spending on war production created millions of jobs, drafted soldiers, and stimulated the economy to full employment, though the New Deal had provided some relief.

Kondratiev Waves

Economic cycles vary in length and intensity. Some are short lived, while others last for decades. **Kondratiev waves** describe long term economic cycles that span roughly 50 to 60 years and are often driven by major technological or structural changes.

The **Industrial Revolution**, spanning the late 1700s through the mid 1800s, is a classic example. Advances in manufacturing, transportation, and energy fundamentally transformed economies and fueled long term growth.

A more recent example is the **digital revolution**, which began in the late 20th century. Personal computers, the internet, mobile technology, and even artificial intelligence, created entirely new industries, disrupted existing ones, and reshaped global economic systems in ways that continue to unfold.

These long cycles are influenced by **Monetary policy**, **Fiscal policy**, geopolitical developments, and technological innovation. Understanding them helps explain why economies evolve over time rather than remaining static.

Last Thoughts

Economic cycles are a natural feature of modern economies. By understanding how each phase works and why transitions occur, **business owners, marketers, students, and everyday consumers** can make more informed decisions during periods of growth and uncertainty.

The goal is not to predict the future perfectly, but to remain adaptable, manage risk wisely, and recognize opportunities as economic conditions change. With this foundation in place, you are better prepared to understand the broader macroeconomic forces explored throughout the rest of this book.

Chapter 2: Inflation

Inflation is one of those economic forces that quietly affects nearly everyone. From small businesses to large corporations, and from households to governments, inflation changes how far money goes and how decisions are made. Over time, it causes goods and services to become more expensive, meaning the same amount of money buys less than it once did, this phenomenon can also be referred to as **currency devaluation**.

Understanding inflation matters because it shapes pricing, wages, interest rates, and purchasing behavior across the entire economy. This chapter explains what inflation is, why it happens, and how it influences both business decisions and everyday life.

What Is Inflation and Why Does It Happen?

At its core, **inflation** refers to a sustained rise in prices throughout an economy over time. As prices increase, the **purchasing power** of money declines. For example, if inflation runs at 5 percent per year, an item that costs $100 today will cost $105 next year.

Inflation does not occur randomly. It develops from identifiable economic pressures that affect supply, demand, costs, and monetary conditions.

Causes of Inflation

Demand Pull Inflation

Demand pull inflation occurs when demand for goods and services grows faster than the economy's ability to supply them. This often happens during strong economic expansions when employment is high and incomes are rising.

When many consumers and businesses compete for a limited supply of products, sellers gain pricing power. A common example is a highly sought after product with limited availability, where increased demand allows prices to rise.

Cost Push Inflation

Cost push inflation happens when the cost of producing goods and services increases and businesses pass those higher costs on to consumers. Rising expenses for raw materials, labor, energy, or transportation can all contribute.

For example, when oil prices increase, shipping and manufacturing costs rise across many industries. Businesses often respond by raising prices to protect profit margins.

Built In Inflation

Built in inflation develops when businesses and workers expect prices to continue rising. Workers may demand higher wages to keep up with living costs, while businesses raise prices to offset higher payroll expenses.

This process creates a feedback loop where expectations of inflation help sustain inflation itself.

Monetary Policy and Excess Money Supply

Monetary policy, controlled by central banks such as the Federal Reserve in the United States, plays a major role in inflation. When central banks lower interest rates or expand the money supply, borrowing and spending typically increase.

While these actions can support economic growth, they can also contribute to inflation if too much money enters the economy without a corresponding increase in goods and services.

Fiscal Policy

Fiscal policy, which includes government spending and taxation decisions, also influences inflation. Tax cuts can boost consumer spending, while large public spending programs can increase demand across the economy.

Even policies that affect the labor force, such as immigration rules, can influence inflation by shaping production capacity and wage pressures. In general, when demand expands faster than supply, upward pressure on prices follows.

Who Is Causing Inflation?

Inflation is often blamed on a single group, but in reality, it results from the combined actions of multiple participants within the economy.

Central banks and governments influence inflation through monetary and fiscal decisions. During economic slowdowns, policymakers may stimulate demand through spending, or lower interest rates. If these efforts overshoot, inflation can rise.

Supply chain disruptions also play a significant role. Events such as pandemics, geopolitical conflicts, or natural disasters can reduce the availability of goods and materials, pushing prices higher.

Businesses and wages contribute as well. Companies that raise wages to attract or retain workers may face higher costs, which are often passed on to consumers through higher prices.

Consumers themselves influence inflation when they rush to buy goods in anticipation of higher prices. This behavior increases demand and can accelerate price increases.

Inflation reflects the interaction of markets, policies, and expectations, rather than the actions of any single group.

The Impact of Inflation on Pricing and Purchasing Power

Inflation creates difficult trade offs for businesses and consumers alike. Rising costs for materials, labor, and operations often force businesses to reconsider pricing strategies. At the same time, consumers facing higher expenses for essentials such as housing, food, and energy may reduce discretionary spending.

As inflation rises, **purchasing power** declines. Households may cut back on dining out, travel, or nonessential purchases. For businesses, this can result in fewer sales, smaller order sizes, or increased competition from lower priced alternatives.

Maintaining profitability without losing customer trust becomes a central challenge. Raising prices too aggressively risks pushing customers away, while absorbing higher costs can strain financial stability.

Sneakflation and Shrinkflation

In response to inflation, some businesses adopt cost saving strategies that are not always immediately obvious to consumers.

Sneakflation refers to maintaining the same price while reducing the overall value of a product or service. This may involve using lower quality materials, reducing customer service benefits, or tightening return policies.

Shrinkflation occurs when product sizes decrease without a corresponding price reduction. This practice has been observed across industries such as packaged foods, beverages, fast food, and household goods.

Both practices highlight how inflation can subtly reshape consumer experiences and business behavior over time.

Last Thoughts

Inflation is a persistent feature of modern economies, and while it can create challenges, it also reveals how adaptable businesses and consumers can be. Understanding inflation allows individuals and organizations to respond strategically rather than react emotionally.

While inflation cannot always be avoided, thoughtful planning, clear communication, and a focus on delivering value can help maintain trust during uncertain periods. How businesses and policymakers respond to inflation often matters as much as inflation itself.

With this foundation, you are better prepared to understand how inflation interacts with economic cycles, policy decisions, and the broader macroeconomic environment explored throughout the rest of this book.

Chapter 3: Tariffs and Trade Agreements

Global economics can feel like a complex puzzle, but understanding it comes with significant rewards. For businesses operating beyond their home country, international markets introduce additional forces such as **exchange rates**, **tariffs**, **trade agreements**, and varying economic conditions across regions.

These forces shape pricing, competitiveness, hiring decisions, and long term strategy. In this chapter, we explore how global trade works in practice, why it is controversial, and how businesses can navigate international markets without relying on oversimplified economic assumptions.

The Role of Exchange Rates: How Currency Fluctuations Impact Business

Exchange rates determine how much one currency is worth relative to another. They fluctuate constantly due to factors such as economic growth, interest rates, inflation, capital flows, and geopolitical events. For businesses engaged in international trade, these movements directly affect pricing and profitability.

Consider a U.S. based business selling products in Europe. If the exchange rate shifts from 1 USD equaling 0.9 EUR to 1 USD equaling 1.1 EUR (for illustration only), the product becomes more expensive for European buyers. Without pricing adjustments, demand may fall.

If the exchange rate moves in the opposite direction, the product becomes cheaper abroad, potentially increasing demand. However, when foreign earnings are converted back into dollars, profit margins may shrink. This is why experienced businesses monitor exchange rate trends closely and often use **hedging**, financial tools designed to lock in favorable rates and reduce uncertainty.

Tariffs: The Hidden Costs and Controversies of International Trade

Tariffs are taxes placed on imported goods, often justified as a way to protect domestic industries from foreign competition. In theory, tariffs make imported products more expensive, encouraging consumers to buy locally produced alternatives.

For businesses heavily dependent on global supply chains, tariffs can introduce challenges, especially if they are not positioned for domestic sourcing or production. A company exporting goods into a country with high tariffs may suddenly find its products priced out of the market unless it adapts its strategy.

Tariffs protect local jobs, preserve strategic industries, and strengthen national economic resilience. For example, imposing tariffs on imported steel can make domestically produced steel more competitive, supporting local manufacturers and workers.

However, tariffs also raise costs for businesses that rely on imported inputs. Higher production costs are often passed along through higher prices, though this does not automatically mean consumers are harmed in every case. Consumers can adjust behavior, choose alternatives, or simply avoid products that no longer provide value.

This is where many economic debates oversimplify the issue. Higher tariffs do not uniformly hurt consumers, but they do expose **poorly positioned businesses**. Companies that lack pricing flexibility, operational efficiency, or strategic alternatives often struggle to compete when tariffs increase. Businesses unable to adapt are more likely to fail, while stronger, better positioned firms adjust.

For example, a company manufacturing electronics may depend on imported microchips or rare earth metals. If tariffs raise input costs, the company faces a decision: raise prices, redesign products, seek alternative suppliers, or shift production domestically. The ripple effects extend far beyond the targeted industry, but the outcomes vary based on business strategy, not just tariff policy.

At their core, tariffs create **winners and losers**. Some industries benefit from reduced competition, while others face higher costs and reduced access to markets. The real impact depends on how businesses respond and how flexible consumers are.

Free Trade: Not Always the Golden Solution

Free trade agreements aim to reduce barriers such as tariffs and quotas, allowing goods and services to move more freely across borders. While often presented as universally beneficial, their real world outcomes are far more complex.

The **North American Free Trade Agreement (NAFTA)** is a clear example. Supporters point to increased trade volumes and economic integration across the U.S., Canada, and Mexico. While in reality, the agreement accelerated the outsourcing of manufacturing jobs from higher wage regions to lower wage ones, leaving many workers and small producers behind.

Agricultural sectors and small businesses often faced intense competition, sometimes forcing local producers out of business. These effects were uneven, benefiting some regions and industries while harming others.

A similar debate surrounds **President Richard Nixon's 1972 visit to China**, which opened the door to expanded trade and eventually lower tariffs. Many economists credit this shift with helping create a modern, technology driven corporate economy focused on higher wage, white collar jobs.

However, this transition also contributed to wage stagnation in traditional manufacturing roles and encouraged companies to shift production overseas. The long term result was a hollowing out of certain domestic industries.

Importantly, the move toward credential based, professional employment also widened existing inequalities. Jobs increasingly required degrees and certifications that were historically less accessible to minority groups, worsening an already present racial wealth gap. This aspect is often ignored in mainstream economic discussions of free trade.

These examples show that while free trade can lower costs and expand markets, it is not a universal solution. It reshapes labor markets, redistributes income, and creates structural changes that benefit some groups while disadvantaging others.

Navigating International Markets with an Economic Perspective

Succeeding internationally requires more than exporting products. Businesses must understand local economic conditions, cultural norms, and regulatory environments.

Evaluating **economic stability** is a starting point. Inflation, unemployment, and consumer spending patterns signal how much purchasing power exists in a market. In high inflation environments, consumers may prioritize affordability, forcing businesses to adjust product size, pricing, or bundling strategies.

Cultural factors also matter. Some economies emphasize saving and long term security, while others reward visible consumption. Products and marketing strategies that succeed in one region may fail in another.

Legal and regulatory structures further complicate decisions. Trade agreements, environmental standards, labor laws, and tax policies vary widely. A country with strict environmental rules may require changes to packaging or sourcing, while relaxed trade barriers may offer cost advantages.

Real World Examples: Adapting to Economic Environments

A business entering a country with high tariffs may choose to establish **local production**, avoiding import duties while creating jobs and goodwill within the host economy.

In markets with volatile exchange rates, businesses may hedge currency exposure or price products in local currency to stabilize revenue.

In high inflation regions, companies often adjust by offering smaller product sizes, value focused bundles, or alternative pricing models to preserve demand.

A recent U.S. example involves the **De Minimis Exemption**, which allowed goods under $800 to enter the country without duties. As this exemption was reduced, many businesses experienced higher costs, effectively facing a new form of tariff pressure.

Some businesses responded by shifting toward domestic production, streamlining supply chains, or using **Foreign Trade Zones (FTZs)** to delay or reduce duty payments and improve cash flow. These adjustments highlight how policy changes can quickly reshape business strategy.

This example reinforces a key point: relying on free trade rules alone is risky. Trade policies can change due to political pressure, cultural shifts, or national priorities. Businesses that fail to plan for these realities expose themselves to unnecessary risk.

Last Thoughts

Global trade shapes nearly every modern business decision. **Exchange rates**, **tariffs**, and **trade agreements** are not abstract theories, they are real forces that influence costs, competitiveness, and survival.

While exchange rates require ongoing monitoring and risk management, tariffs and free trade demand a deeper understanding of their trade offs. They reward preparation and adaptability, not blind optimism.

Businesses that recognize these realities, stay informed, and position themselves strategically are far better equipped to navigate international markets and pursue sustainable growth in an increasingly complex global economy.

Chapter 4: Economic Indicators

Data, **forecasting**, and **market trends** are the tools businesses and policymakers use to understand what is happening now, anticipate what may happen next, and identify patterns that shape economic behavior. Economic data, often called **economic indicators**, provides measurable signals such as inflation rates, unemployment figures, and production levels.

Forecasting uses that data to project future demand, costs, and risks. **Market trends** reveal longer term shifts in consumer behavior, technology, and economic structure. When used together, these tools help decision makers reduce uncertainty, plan strategically, and act before changes fully show up in the broader economy.

CPI and PCE: Tracking the Cost of Living

The **Consumer Price Index (CPI)** measures the average change in prices consumers pay for a fixed basket of goods and services over time. It is often described as a cost of living tracker, covering items such as food, housing, transportation, and healthcare.

CPI is widely used to measure **inflation**, meaning rising prices that reduce purchasing power. For businesses, a rising CPI may signal higher operating costs and more price sensitive customers. Common responses include emphasizing value, adjusting product offerings, or reducing expenses.

However, CPI has well known limitations. Because it tracks a fixed basket of goods, it does not fully reflect how consumers change behavior when prices rise, such as switching to cheaper alternatives. This can cause CPI to overstate or misrepresent real inflation pressures.

For this reason, the Federal Reserve prefers the **Personal Consumption Expenditures (PCE) Price Index**, along with **Core PCE**, which excludes food and energy prices. PCE adjusts for changing consumer behavior and provides a broader view of spending patterns. Core PCE is considered especially useful for policy decisions because food and energy prices tend to fluctuate sharply.

GDP: The Economy's Scorecard, With Caveats

Again, **Gross Domestic Product (GDP)** measures the total value of all goods and services produced within a country. It is commonly used to determine whether an economy is growing or contracting.

A rising GDP often signals strong economic activity and may encourage businesses to invest, hire, or expand. However, GDP has serious limitations. Its calculation methods have changed over time, making long term comparisons difficult. Some modern GDP figures even include estimates for underground or illegal activity in certain countries.

More importantly, GDP does not reflect income inequality, unpaid labor, or overall quality of life. It is also heavily influenced by **government spending**, which can artificially inflate growth without creating sustainable economic value. For this reason, **real GDP**, which adjusts for inflation, is often more useful, but still incomplete.

A strong GDP number does not always mean the economy is healthy for households or small businesses.

Unemployment Rates: The Labor Market's Pulse

The **unemployment rate** measures the percentage of people in the labor force who are actively seeking work but cannot find it. Low unemployment is often viewed as a sign of economic strength, while high unemployment signals economic stress.

However, unemployment data has weaknesses. It excludes discouraged workers who stop looking for jobs, undercounts long term unemployed individuals, and ignores underemployment, such as part time workers who want full time jobs.

Because of this, unemployment rates should never be viewed in isolation.

Labor Force Participation Rate: What Unemployment Misses

The **labor force participation rate** shows the percentage of working age individuals who are either employed or actively seeking work. This indicator helps reveal whether people are exiting the workforce entirely.

A declining participation rate can indicate structural issues such as skill mismatches, demographic shifts, or long term discouragement. Even when unemployment appears low, a weak participation rate may suggest underlying labor market problems.

For businesses, this can signal hiring challenges. For marketers and policymakers, it affects consumer demand and long term growth potential.

Balance of Trade: Deficits, Surpluses, and Strategy

The **balance of trade** measures the difference between a country's exports and imports. A **trade surplus** occurs when exports exceed imports, while a **trade deficit** occurs when imports outweigh exports.

Trade deficits are often framed as economic weaknesses, but their impact depends on context. Persistent deficits may increase reliance on foreign supply chains and expose businesses to tariffs or currency risk. However, they can also reflect strong domestic consumption.

Tracking trade data helps businesses anticipate supply chain pressures, pricing risks, and international competition.

Interest Rates: The Price of Time and Risk

Interest rates, influenced by central banks, represent the cost of borrowing and the reward for saving. They directly affect mortgages, business loans, credit cards, and investment decisions.

Low interest rates encourage borrowing and spending, which can stimulate growth but also fuel inflation. High rates discourage borrowing, slow demand, and are often used to control inflation.

Interest rates influence nearly every economic indicator discussed in this chapter.

Yield Curve: A Quiet Recession Signal

The **yield curve** compares short term and long term interest rates on government bonds. Under normal conditions, long term rates are higher than short term rates.

When the yield curve **inverts**, meaning short term rates exceed long term rates, it has historically preceded recessions. This happens because investors expect slower growth and lower future interest rates.

The yield curve does not predict timing precisely, but it provides valuable insight into expectations, credit conditions, and policy credibility.

Consumer Confidence Index: The Psychology of Spending

The **Consumer Confidence Index (CCI)** measures how optimistic consumers feel about the economy, job prospects, and personal finances.

High confidence often leads to increased spending, while low confidence encourages saving and caution. However, sentiment can be influenced by media narratives, politics, or short term price shocks.

Confidence matters because perception often drives behavior, even when economic fundamentals lag behind.

Producer Price Index: Inflation Before It Reaches Consumers

The **Producer Price Index (PPI)** tracks price changes received by producers rather than consumers. It reflects upstream inflation pressures in manufacturing and services.

Rising PPI may indicate future consumer inflation, though not all cost increases are passed along. Some businesses absorb higher costs, which can compress margins instead.

PPI is most useful as an early warning signal rather than a direct consumer price predictor.

Housing Starts and Building Permits: A Ground Level Indicator

Housing starts and **building permits** track new residential construction activity. Housing reflects interest rates, labor availability, material costs, and consumer confidence all at once.

When housing activity slows, it often signals tightening credit conditions or weakening demand. When it accelerates, it can indicate economic expansion.

Housing is especially important because it influences employment, local economies, and consumer spending far beyond construction itself.

Purchasing Managers' Index: Early Signals from Supply Chains

The **Purchasing Managers' Index (PMI)** surveys managers on production, new orders, employment, inventories, and supplier deliveries.

A PMI above 50 signals expansion, while below 50 signals contraction. PMI is forward looking but sentiment driven, meaning it can exaggerate trends during periods of uncertainty.

Even with its limitations, PMI provides early insight into economic momentum.

Stock Market Indices: Sentiment, Not Reality

Stock indices such as the **S&P 500**, **Dow Jones**, **Russell 2000**, and **Nasdaq** reflect investor expectations and corporate earnings outlooks.

They are not the economy itself. Markets can rise while wages stagnate or small businesses struggle. Indices are best viewed as sentiment indicators rather than comprehensive measures of economic health.

Precious Metals: A Market Based Economic Indicator

Precious metals, especially **gold and silver**, have long been viewed as informal economic indicators. Unlike government reported data, precious metals prices are shaped largely by market behavior, investor psychology, and global capital flows. This makes them useful for understanding how people *feel* about economic conditions, even when official indicators suggest stability.

Gold and silver do not measure economic output or employment directly. Instead, they often reflect **confidence**, **risk perception**, and **trust in financial systems**. When investors become concerned about inflation, currency stability, or geopolitical risk, demand for precious metals often rises.

Last Thoughts

Economic indicators are tools, not truths. Each metric captures only part of the economic picture and often reflects assumptions built into its methodology.

The real value comes from **combining indicators**, questioning their limitations, and pairing them with real world observation and internal data. When used thoughtfully, economic indicators help you respond strategically rather than react emotionally.

The goal is not perfect prediction. It is informed decision making in an uncertain world.

Chapter 5: Economic Schools of Thought

When it comes to understanding economics, there is no single framework that explains everything. Over time, different **economic schools of thought** have developed, each offering a distinct way of interpreting markets, government intervention, and human behavior.

For students, these schools provide the intellectual foundation of economics. For business owners, executives, and even politicians, they shape assumptions about growth, risk, and strategy. For marketers, they help explain why consumers behave the way they do, especially under changing economic conditions.

This chapter explores the major schools of economic thought, **Classical**, **Keynesian**, **Monetarist**, **Austrian**, and **Behavioral**, and explains how each perspective still influences modern policy, business decisions, and consumer behavior.

Classical Economics: The Power of Free Markets

Classical economics, most closely associated with **Adam Smith** and **David Ricardo**, is built on the idea that markets function best when they are allowed to operate freely with minimal government interference.

At the center of this school is the concept of the **invisible hand**, the idea that individuals acting in their own self interest unintentionally promote efficiency and benefit society as a whole. When buyers and sellers interact freely, prices adjust naturally, supply meets demand, and resources flow to their most productive uses.

Classical economists believe that:

- Markets are largely **self correcting**
- Competition drives efficiency and innovation
- Government intervention often creates distortions and unintended consequences

This school of thought laid the foundation for **capitalism** and continues to influence debates around deregulation, taxation, and free trade. For businesses, classical economics supports strategies focused on efficiency, competition, and long term market driven growth.

However, classical theory assumes rational behavior and smooth market adjustments, assumptions that later schools would challenge.

Keynesian Economics: Demand Drives Growth

Keynesian economics, developed by **John Maynard Keynes** during the Great Depression, emerged as a direct challenge to classical thinking.

Keynes argued that markets do not always self correct quickly, especially during economic downturns. When confidence collapses, consumers stop spending and businesses stop investing, creating a vicious cycle of falling demand, rising unemployment, and economic stagnation.

Keynesians believe that:

- **Aggregate demand** is the primary driver of economic growth
- During recessions, private markets may fail to recover on their own
- Government intervention is sometimes necessary to stabilize the economy

Through **fiscal policy**, such as public spending, tax cuts, or stimulus programs, governments can inject demand into the economy and restore confidence. This approach has been widely used during crises, including the **2008 financial crisis** and the **COVID 19 pandemic**.

For businesses, Keynesian economics explains why government spending can temporarily support sales and employment, but also why excessive reliance on stimulus may create longer term inflation or debt concerns.

Monetarism: Controlling the Money Supply

Monetarism, most closely associated with **Milton Friedman**, places primary emphasis on the role of money in the economy.

Friedman argued that **inflation** is fundamentally a monetary phenomenon. When too much money circulates relative to the supply of goods and services, prices rise. From this perspective, economic instability is often caused by poor control of the money supply rather than insufficient demand.

Additionally, Friedman also argued that **Gresham's Law**, an economic principle which states that "bad money drives out good money". Can lead to individuals using cheaper, less valuable money for everyday transactions (credit lines, and cryptocurrency) while saving or exporting the more valuable money (cash and precious metals), which has a higher opportunity cost. This leads to the eventual disappearance of "good money" from active circulation. Which can lead to currency instability and inflation.

Key monetarist beliefs include:

- Stable growth in the money supply promotes long term stability
- Central banks play a critical role in managing inflation, and currency devaluation
- Excessive government spending can worsen inflationary pressures, and currency devaluation

Rather than relying on large scale fiscal intervention, monetarists favor predictable and disciplined **monetary policy**, using tools such as interest rates and liquidity controls.

This school gained prominence during the high inflation period of the 1970s and continues to influence central bank decision making today, particularly in debates around inflation control versus economic growth.

Austrian Economics: Individual Choice and Market Corrections

Austrian economics, rooted in the work of **Carl Menger**, **Ludwig von Mises**, and **Friedrich Hayek**, focuses heavily on **individual choice**, entrepreneurship, and decentralized decision making.

Austrians are deeply skeptical of government intervention, arguing that markets are complex systems driven by dispersed knowledge that no central authority can fully understand or manage. From this perspective, policies that manipulate interest rates or inject artificial stimulus distort price signals and encourage inefficient investment.

Key Austrian principles include:

- Markets evolve organically through human action
- Recessions are natural corrections to prior excesses
- Government intervention often delays recovery and worsens misallocation

Austrian economists view economic downturns not as failures, but as necessary resets that clear out inefficiencies. For entrepreneurs and business owners, this school emphasizes adaptability, risk awareness, and the dangers of relying too heavily on policy support.

Behavioral Economics: Humans Are Not Fully Rational

Behavioral economics represents a major departure from traditional economic assumptions. Instead of assuming people always act rationally, it incorporates insights from psychology to explain how real humans actually behave.

Behavioral economists study how **biases**, **emotions**, and **mental shortcuts** influence decision making. Concepts such as **loss aversion**, **anchoring**, **overconfidence**, and **herd behavior** help explain why markets sometimes behave irrationally.

Key insights from behavioral economics include:

- People fear losses more than they value equivalent gains
- Decisions are influenced by framing and context
- Consumers often act emotionally rather than logically

This school is especially useful for marketers and business owners. Pricing strategies, promotions, branding, and messaging all rely heavily on behavioral insights. Behavioral economics also helps explain bubbles, panic selling, and why consumers sometimes ignore long term benefits in favor of short term comfort.

Importantly, behavioral economics challenges the idea that markets always self correct efficiently, reinforcing why sentiment and confidence matter so much in macroeconomic cycles.

Why No Economic School Gets It Completely Right

One of the biggest mistakes people make when learning economics is treating any single school of thought as a complete answer. In reality, **no economic framework fully explains how economies behave at all times**. Each school highlights certain truths while downplaying others.

Classical economics assumes markets are efficient and self correcting, but history shows markets can stay irrational longer than expected. Keynesian economics explains short term demand shocks well, yet prolonged intervention can distort incentives and fuel inflation. Monetarism correctly emphasizes money supply, but it often underestimates how human behavior and global shocks affect outcomes.

Austrian economics values discipline and entrepreneurship, but its hands off approach can ignore real world hardship during deep downturns. Behavioral economics explains decision making brilliantly, but it does not always offer clear policy solutions.

The economy is not a controlled laboratory. It is a **dynamic system shaped by incentives, psychology, politics, culture, and timing**. Policies that work in one decade may fail in another. Strategies that succeed in one country may collapse in another.

This is why economic debates are often so heated. People are not just arguing about data, they are arguing about **assumptions**. What you assume about human behavior, government competence, and market efficiency determines which school of thought you favor.

For business owners and marketers, this matters deeply. Blindly following economic narratives can lead to poor decisions. Expansion during stimulus fueled booms can backfire. Overconfidence in free trade can expose supply chain fragility. Overreliance on government support can weaken long term resilience.

The most effective decision makers borrow selectively. They understand **when markets work**, **when intervention matters**, **when money supply dominates**, and **when psychology overrides logic**.

Economic literacy is not about loyalty to an ideology. It is about recognizing patterns, questioning assumptions, and adapting as conditions change.

Last Thoughts

No single school of economic thought explains the economy perfectly. Each offers valuable insights, while also carrying limitations.

To summarize:

- **Classical economics** emphasizes free markets and efficiency
- **Keynesian economics** highlights demand and government intervention
- **Monetarism** focuses on money supply and inflation control
- **Austrian economics** prioritizes individual choice and market discipline
- **Behavioral economics** explains the psychological side of decision making

Understanding these perspectives is not about choosing a single ideology. It is about recognizing when each framework applies and using them together to make better decisions.

Chapter 6: Monetary Policy and Central Banks

Monetary policy is one of the most powerful, and often misunderstood, forces in the economy. While it operates mostly behind the scenes, its effects show up everywhere, from interest rates and inflation to employment, asset prices, and consumer confidence.

At the center of monetary policy are **central banks**, institutions tasked with managing the supply of money and credit in an economy. For businesses, marketers, students, and everyday consumers, understanding how central banks operate helps explain why borrowing suddenly becomes more expensive, why inflation accelerates or slows, and why economic conditions can change quickly even without new legislation.

This chapter breaks down what monetary policy is, how central banks use it, and why it matters in the real world.

What Is Monetary Policy?

Monetary policy refers to the actions taken by a central bank to influence economic activity by controlling the availability and cost of money. The primary goals of monetary policy typically include:

- Controlling **inflation**
- Supporting **employment**
- Promoting overall **economic stability**

In the United States, these responsibilities fall to the **Federal Reserve**, often referred to as the Fed. Other countries have their own central banks, such as the European Central Bank and the Bank of England, but the core tools and objectives are similar.

Unlike fiscal policy, which involves government spending and taxation, monetary policy works through financial systems, banks, and credit markets.

The Role of Central Banks

Central banks serve as the backbone of modern financial systems. Their responsibilities extend beyond simply setting interest rates.

Key roles of central banks include:

- Managing inflation expectations
- Acting as a lender of last resort during financial crises
- Regulating and stabilizing banking systems
- Influencing credit conditions and liquidity

Central banks aim to balance economic growth with price stability. When this balance breaks down, inflation, recessions, or financial instability often follow.

Importantly, central banks operate with a degree of independence from elected governments. This independence is intended to prevent short term political pressures from driving long term economic damage, though in practice, this separation is often tested.

Interest Rates: The Primary Lever

The most visible tool of monetary policy is the **interest rate**.

When central banks **lower interest rates**, borrowing becomes cheaper. Businesses are more likely to invest, consumers are more willing to spend, and economic activity tends to increase. However, if rates remain too low for too long, inflation and asset bubbles can form.

When central banks **raise interest rates**, borrowing becomes more expensive. Spending slows, inflationary pressures ease, and economic growth cools. While this can help stabilize prices, it can also slow hiring and increase the risk of recession.

Interest rates influence nearly every part of the economy, including mortgages, credit cards, business loans, stock valuations, and even currency exchange rates.

Money Supply and Liquidity

Beyond interest rates, central banks also manage the **money supply**, the amount of money circulating in the economy.

When central banks increase liquidity, more money is available for lending and spending. When they restrict liquidity, credit becomes tighter and economic activity slows.

Modern central banking focuses less on physically printing money and more on influencing how easily money flows through financial institutions. This distinction is important, as inflation is often driven by **credit expansion**, not just cash creation.

Quantitative Easing and Tightening

During extreme economic stress, central banks may use unconventional tools.

Quantitative easing (QE) involves purchasing large quantities of financial assets, such as government bonds, to inject liquidity into the economy. QE is designed to lower long term interest rates, support financial markets, and encourage lending.

QE played a major role following the **2008 financial crisis** and again during the **COVID 19 pandemic**. While it helped stabilize markets, it also contributed to asset price inflation and raised concerns about long term distortions.

The opposite process, **quantitative tightening (QT)**, involves reducing central bank balance sheets by selling assets or allowing them to mature. QT aims to remove excess liquidity and control inflation, but it can also tighten financial conditions rapidly.

These tools highlight how powerful, and risky, monetary policy can be when pushed to extremes.

Monetary Policy and Inflation

One of the central bank's primary responsibilities is controlling **inflation**.

When inflation rises too quickly, central banks typically tighten policy by raising interest rates and reducing liquidity. When inflation is low or economic growth weakens, they may ease policy to stimulate demand.

Again, inflation is not always caused by monetary factors alone. Supply chain disruptions, energy shocks, and geopolitical events can all drive prices higher, sometimes beyond the immediate control of central banks.

This creates a difficult challenge. Tightening policy too aggressively can slow the economy unnecessarily, while acting too slowly can allow inflation expectations to become entrenched.

Monetary Policy and Employment

Central banks also influence **employment**, though indirectly.

Lower interest rates can encourage businesses to expand and hire, while higher rates often lead companies to pause investment and reduce hiring. However, monetary policy cannot directly create jobs or fix structural labor issues.

This limitation is often overlooked. Monetary policy works best when paired with sound fiscal policy and a productive economic environment. Expecting central banks alone to manage growth, inflation, and employment places unrealistic pressure on monetary tools.

Limitations and Criticisms of Monetary Policy

While powerful, monetary policy is not a cure all.

Critics argue that prolonged low interest rates distort markets, encourage excessive risk taking (moral hazard), and widen wealth inequality by inflating asset prices. Others point out that monetary policy often benefits large financial institutions first, with delayed effects for households and small businesses (trickle down effect).

There is also the issue of timing. Monetary policy operates with **lags**, meaning decisions made today may not fully affect the economy for months or even years. This makes precision extremely difficult.

Central banks are often forced to act with incomplete data, imperfect indicators, and political pressure, increasing the risk of policy mistakes.

Why Monetary Policy Matters for Businesses and Consumers

For businesses, monetary policy influences:

- Borrowing costs
- Expansion timing
- Pricing strategies
- Consumer demand

For consumers, it affects:

- Mortgage and loan rates
- Credit access
- Job opportunities
- Cost of living

Understanding central bank behavior helps individuals and businesses avoid being surprised by rapid shifts in economic conditions.

Last Thoughts

Monetary policy shapes the economic environment more quietly than fiscal policy, but its effects are far reaching. Central banks influence inflation, credit, employment, and financial stability, often with a single policy decision.

While monetary tools can stabilize economies during crises, they are not without trade offs. Overuse can distort markets, while underuse can allow instability to grow.

The key takeaway is not blind trust or rejection of central banking, but awareness. Understanding how monetary policy works allows you to interpret economic shifts more clearly, plan more strategically, and make decisions grounded in reality rather than headlines.

Chapter 7: Fiscal Policy and Government Spending

While monetary policy works through banks and financial markets, **fiscal policy** operates much more visibly. It shows up in government budgets, stimulus programs, taxes, public services, and national debt discussions. Fiscal policy is often where economics and politics collide, making it one of the most debated forces in the economy.

For businesses, marketers, and everyday consumers, fiscal policy affects disposable income, demand, employment opportunities, and long term economic stability. Understanding how government spending and taxation work helps explain why certain industries boom, why deficits grow, and why economic outcomes often differ from political promises.

This chapter explains what fiscal policy is, how it is used, and why it produces both intended and unintended consequences.

What Is Fiscal Policy?

Fiscal policy refers to government decisions about **spending**, **taxation**, and **borrowing**. These decisions influence economic activity by shaping how much money flows through the economy and where it is directed.

Governments use fiscal policy to:

- Stimulate economic growth
- Reduce unemployment
- Support specific industries or populations
- Respond to recessions or emergencies

Unlike monetary policy, which is managed by central banks, fiscal policy is created through legislative and executive processes, making it slower, more political, and often less precise.

Government Spending: Stimulus and Support

Government spending can take many forms, including:

- Infrastructure projects

- Social programs
- Defense spending
- Education and healthcare funding
- Direct payments or subsidies

During economic downturns, governments often increase spending to stimulate demand. This approach aligns with **Keynesian economics**, which argues that public spending can offset declines in private sector activity.

Large scale spending can boost employment and stabilize demand in the short term. However, it can also create inefficiencies if funds are misallocated or if spending continues long after emergency conditions have passed.

For businesses, government spending can create opportunities, especially in industries tied to public contracts or infrastructure. At the same time, it can distort competition by favoring certain sectors over others.

Taxation: Incentives and Trade Offs

Taxes influence behavior as much as they generate revenue. Changes in tax policy affect:

- Consumer spending
- Business investment
- Hiring decisions
- Capital allocation

Lower taxes can increase disposable income and encourage investment, while higher taxes may reduce spending or push businesses to adjust pricing and operations.

However, tax cuts do not always lead to productive growth. When tax reductions primarily benefit asset holders rather than productive investment, the economic impact may be limited or uneven.

From a macro perspective, taxation is less about fairness debates and more about **incentives**. How taxes are structured often matters more than how much is collected.

Budget Deficits and National Debt

When government spending exceeds revenue, the result is a **budget deficit**. Persistent deficits accumulate into **national debt**.

Deficits are often framed as inherently negative, but context matters. During recessions or emergencies, deficit spending can stabilize the economy. Over the long term, however, sustained deficits raise concerns about debt sustainability, inflation risk, and future tax burdens.

High debt levels can limit policy flexibility, especially if interest costs rise. As debt servicing consumes more resources, governments may face pressure to cut spending, raise taxes, or rely more heavily on monetary intervention.

For businesses and consumers, rising debt can eventually translate into higher taxes, reduced services, or inflationary pressures.

Fiscal Policy and Inflation

Fiscal policy plays a direct role in **inflation**, especially when spending expands faster than the economy's productive capacity.

Large spending programs, subsidies, or transfers can increase demand quickly. If supply cannot keep pace, prices rise. This dynamic becomes especially pronounced when fiscal stimulus overlaps with loose monetary policy.

While fiscal spending can support recovery, prolonged or poorly timed stimulus risks overheating the economy. Inflation is often the delayed cost of aggressive fiscal expansion.

Targeted Spending and Economic Distortions

Governments often use fiscal policy to support specific industries, regions, or groups. While targeted spending can address short term problems, it can also distort markets.

Subsidies may keep inefficient firms alive, delay innovation, or discourage competition. Regulations tied to spending programs can increase compliance costs for businesses.

These distortions do not always show up immediately, but over time they can reduce productivity and slow growth.

Fiscal Policy During Crises

Fiscal policy is most defensible during emergencies. Natural disasters, financial crises, and pandemics often require rapid government response.

Programs introduced during crises are often labeled temporary, but many persist long after conditions normalize. This creates structural spending commitments that are difficult to unwind politically.

The long term challenge is distinguishing between **emergency support** and **permanent expansion**, a line that is rarely clean in practice.

Why Governments Struggle to Reverse Spending

Once government spending expands, it becomes very difficult to reverse. This is not necessarily because the spending was unjustified at the start, but because **economic, political, and institutional incentives favor permanence over rollback**.

Programs introduced during crises are often framed as temporary solutions. In practice, they quickly become embedded in budgets, contracts, and expectations. Businesses adapt to them, workers depend on them, and agencies are built to administer them. Removing the spending later feels less like policy adjustment and more like disruption.

Political incentives reinforce this pattern. Cutting spending creates immediate, visible pain, while the benefits of fiscal restraint are long term and diffuse. As a result, elected officials face strong pressure to maintain or expand programs rather than reduce them, even when conditions have changed.

There is also a feedback loop between spending and economic expectations. Once markets and households assume ongoing government support, removing it can trigger uncertainty or slowdowns. This often leads policymakers to delay or abandon efforts to unwind stimulus, reinforcing dependence on fiscal intervention.

This dynamic helps explain why **temporary spending becomes structural**, why deficits persist across economic cycles, and why fiscal discipline is politically difficult even during periods of growth.

Understanding this reality matters for businesses and consumers. It shapes tax policy, inflation risk, regulatory complexity, and long term economic flexibility. Governments rarely struggle to create programs. They struggle to end them.

Limitations and Criticisms of Fiscal Policy

Fiscal policy faces several structural challenges:

- Political incentives often favor short term benefits over long term stability
- Policy changes take time to implement
- Spending efficiency varies widely
- Debt accumulation can limit future options

Unlike monetary policy, fiscal decisions are deeply influenced by elections, lobbying, and public opinion. This makes consistent, disciplined application difficult.

Fiscal policy can be powerful, but it is rarely precise.

Why Fiscal Policy Matters for Businesses and Consumers

For businesses, fiscal policy influences:

- Demand for goods and services
- Tax obligations and incentives
- Regulatory costs
- Long term planning certainty

For consumers, it affects:

- Disposable income
- Employment opportunities
- Public services
- Cost of living

Understanding fiscal policy helps explain why economic conditions often change slowly and why policy outcomes rarely match expectations exactly.

Last Thoughts

Fiscal policy is one of the most visible tools governments use to influence the economy, but visibility does not guarantee effectiveness. Spending and taxation can stabilize growth in the short term while creating long term trade offs.

The key lesson is balance. Strategic fiscal intervention can support economies during stress, but unchecked expansion can weaken resilience and flexibility.

For decision makers at every level, fiscal policy should be viewed as a powerful tool, not a permanent solution. Understanding its limits is just as important as understanding its benefits.

Chapter 8: Employment, Wages, and Productivity

Employment, wages, and productivity sit at the center of how people experience the economy. While GDP, inflation, and policy decisions often dominate headlines, these three forces determine whether households feel stable, stretched, or left behind.

For businesses, they shape hiring decisions, labor costs, and long term competitiveness. For consumers, they determine income, spending power, and financial security. And for policymakers, they represent both economic goals and political pressure points.

This chapter explores how employment, wages, and productivity interact, and why improving one without the others often leads to unintended consequences.

Employment: More Than Just Job Counts

Employment measures how many people are working, but the quality and stability of those jobs matter just as much as the number itself.

Low unemployment is often interpreted as a sign of economic strength. More people earning income generally means higher spending and stronger demand. However, employment figures can hide deeper issues such as:

- Underemployment
- Job insecurity
- Low wage growth
- Declining labor force participation

An economy can appear healthy on paper while workers struggle in practice. This is why employment data must be viewed alongside wage trends and productivity levels.

Wages: Income, Incentives, and Inflation

Wages represent the compensation workers receive for their labor. Rising wages are usually viewed positively, but wage growth does not exist in isolation.

When wages rise because productivity improves, businesses can afford higher pay without raising prices significantly. When wages rise without productivity gains, businesses often respond by increasing prices, cutting staff, or reducing hours.

This dynamic connects wages directly to **inflation**. If higher labor costs are not matched by higher output, prices tend to rise. This is why wage growth can feel empowering for workers in the short term but inflationary for the economy over time.

Wages are also shaped by bargaining power, labor supply, skill availability, and policy decisions. Minimum wage laws, immigration policy, and labor regulations all influence how wages move across industries.

Productivity: The Foundation of Long Term Growth

Productivity measures how much output is produced per unit of labor. In simple terms, it reflects how efficiently work is done.

Productivity growth allows economies to:

- Raise wages sustainably
- Keep prices stable

- Improve living standards
- Compete globally

When productivity stagnates, wage growth becomes harder to sustain without inflation. This is why productivity is often called the engine of long term economic growth.

Advances in technology, education, infrastructure, and management practices all contribute to productivity. However, productivity gains are uneven. Some industries and workers benefit more than others, creating gaps in income and opportunity.

The Employment Wage Productivity Triangle

Employment, wages, and productivity are deeply interconnected. Improving one while ignoring the others often leads to imbalance.

For example:

- High employment without productivity growth can lead to inflation

- Wage increases without productivity gains can strain businesses
- Productivity growth without wage growth can widen inequality

Healthy economies tend to improve all three together over time. When that balance breaks down, economic stress follows.

This is why policy solutions that focus on a single metric often disappoint. Job creation alone does not guarantee prosperity if wages stagnate. Wage growth alone does not guarantee stability if productivity lags.

Policy, Labor Markets, and Trade Offs

Government policy influences labor markets in many ways. **Fiscal policy** affects demand and hiring incentives, while **monetary policy** shapes borrowing conditions for businesses.

Labor regulations, tax incentives, education funding, and immigration policy all affect workforce availability and skill development. These policies involve trade offs. Protecting workers can raise costs for businesses. Encouraging flexibility can reduce security for employees.

There are no perfect solutions, only choices with consequences.

Automation, Technology, and the Changing Workforce

Technological change reshapes employment constantly. Automation and artificial intelligence improve productivity, but they also displace certain jobs.

Over time, new roles emerge, often requiring different skills. This transition can be disruptive, especially for workers without access to retraining or education.

From a macro perspective, technology driven productivity gains are essential for growth. From a human perspective, the transition can be uneven and painful. Ignoring either side leads to poor policy and business decisions.

Why Job Numbers Don't Tell the Whole Story

Headline job numbers are often treated as definitive proof of economic strength, but they rarely capture the full reality of the labor market. While employment data shows how many people are working, it says far less about **job quality**, **income stability**, or **long term opportunity**.

Many jobs created during expansions are part time, temporary, or low wage positions that offer limited security or upward mobility. Others may disappear quickly during downturns. A rising employment count can mask stagnant wages, declining benefits, or increasing reliance on multiple jobs to make ends meet.

Job data also overlooks shifts in **labor force participation**. When people stop looking for work altogether, they no longer appear in unemployment statistics, even though economic stress remains. This can make labor markets appear stronger than they actually are.

Productivity is another missing piece. An economy can add jobs without becoming more productive. In those cases, wage growth becomes harder to sustain without raising prices, contributing to inflation rather than genuine prosperity.

Finally, job numbers do not reflect regional or demographic differences. Certain industries, locations, or groups may thrive while others fall behind. National averages hide these disparities, leading to misleading conclusions about economic health.

This is why employment data should always be viewed alongside wages, productivity, and participation rates. Job creation matters, but **the type of jobs created matters just as much**.

Why Employment, Wages, and Productivity Matter Together

For businesses, these forces influence:

- Hiring and retention
- Pricing decisions
- Investment planning
- Long term competitiveness

For consumers, they determine:

- Income stability
- Purchasing power
- Career mobility

- Quality of life

For the economy as a whole, they shape growth, inflation, and resilience.

Last Thoughts

Employment, wages, and productivity form the backbone of economic well being. Focusing on any one without the others leads to distortion and disappointment.

Sustainable prosperity requires productive work, fair compensation, and meaningful employment opportunities. When these elements move together, economies grow stronger. When they fall out of balance, economic stress becomes unavoidable.

Understanding how these forces interact helps explain why economic outcomes often feel uneven, and why simple solutions rarely work. It also reinforces a central theme of this book, macroeconomics is about systems, not slogans.

Conclusion

Macroeconomics is not about predicting the future with certainty. It is about understanding the **systems, incentives, and trade offs** that shape economic outcomes over time. Throughout this book, you have seen how growth, inflation, trade, policy, labor markets, and human behavior interact in ways that are complex, imperfect, and often misunderstood.

Economic cycles show us that expansions and contractions are not accidents. Inflation reminds us that prices, wages, and money supply are deeply connected. Trade and tariffs reveal that globalization creates winners and losers, not universal prosperity. Economic indicators teach us that data can inform decisions, but never tell the whole story. Schools of thought show that no single framework explains everything. Monetary and fiscal policy demonstrate how powerful tools can stabilize economies, while also creating long term consequences. Employment, wages, and productivity reveal how economic health is ultimately experienced by people, not spreadsheets.

A central theme runs through all of these topics, **economies are dynamic systems, not machines**. They are shaped by policy, incentives, psychology, culture, and timing. Decisions made with good intentions can produce unintended outcomes. Metrics designed to simplify reality can distort it. Short term solutions can create long term challenges.

For students, this understanding builds true economic literacy. Instead of memorizing definitions, you now have a framework for questioning assumptions and interpreting events. For business owners and marketers, this perspective sharpens strategic thinking. It helps you plan beyond headlines, prepare for shifts in demand, and position yourself for resilience rather than reaction. For everyday consumers, it provides clarity in a world where economic news often feels confusing or contradictory.

The goal of macroeconomics is not certainty. It is **context**. When you understand how the pieces fit together, you are less likely to be surprised by change and more capable of adapting when it arrives.

As you move forward, remember this, no indicator tells the full story, no policy works forever, and no economy stands still. The most valuable skill is not prediction, but **understanding**.

That understanding is what allows you to navigate uncertainty with confidence, make better decisions, and see the economy not as something happening to you, but as a system you can learn to interpret and respond to intelligently.

About the Author

Roggie “Raj” Clark is an entrepreneur and a 10-year marketing professional with a proven track record in e-commerce and digital business growth. Having built and managed successful online stores with thousands of sales and consulted for numerous marketing clients, Roggie has mastered the intricacies of online marketing, branding, and consumer behavior. He has also written several popular books on digital marketing, SEO (search engine optimization), and programming (HTML, CSS, and JavaScript).

As a former marketing manager at a fintech company—a role he secured through his own marketing and financial expertise—Roggie gained firsthand experience in financial strategy and wealth-building. This journey inspired him to share insights with amateur investors, helping them save money, make smarter financial decisions, and build long-term wealth. Raj currently lives in Maryland with his sister and niece.

www.ingramcontent.com/pod-product-compliance
Lightning Source LLC
LaVergne TN
LVHW022309200926
848481LV00004B/1251